How to Look at your Depression and Trauma through the Lens of Compassion and Humor

Jen Perry

For more information, email info@staringatwalls.com.

ISBN: 979-8-88759-579-5 - paperback
ISBN: 979-8-88759-580-1 - ebook

CONTENTS

Get Your Free Gift!...vii

Is this book for you?...xi

Preface... xiii

Chapter 1: Depression, Gotta Love it..................................1

Chapter 2: Peeps be Peepin'..5

Chapter 3: Mental Illness and Relationships.....................12

Chapter 4: The Six-Letter F-Word 23

Chapter 5: Helping Others (Maybe) 31

Chapter 6: "Sometimes I Want to Die"
            and Other Lovely Thoughts.............................34

Chapter 7: The Ugliness of Sexual Assault 44

Chapter 8: PTSD, Anxiety and Martial Arts 53

Chapter 9: Interview with my Lover in the Nighttime 60

Conclusion: What Next? 69

Appendix A: Depression Protocol..71

Acknowledgements..75

About the Author 77

Get Your Free Gift

My gift to you is a "Depression Protocol" printout and a whole host of helpful resources located at the below website. Put this protocol on your fridge, fold it up and put it in your journal or tape it above your nightstand. This can be an easy reminder for when you need some extra help to get moving.

You can get a copy and access other helpful resources by visiting: _http://_www.staringatwalls.com.

To Adrienne, who believed in me from the beginning and is my kindred spirit.

Is this book for you?

You could have picked up this book for a number of reasons. Maybe you have depression and are reading every book that has the word "depression" and "trauma" included in case there's a tidbit that will help, or you have a friend or family member that struggles with these issues. Maybe something in the book description spoke to you. Maybe you thought this was a completely different book, but now you're stuck on a 12-hour flight and the internet is broken, so this book it is. Regardless of the reason, I'm so glad you're here. Welcome. Even though I may never meet you, I welcome and accept you. Whatever is going on in your life, take a breath. If you decide to keep reading this conglomeration of rambling thoughts by a slightly-crazy loon, I've got you for as long as you choose to read this book. May you breathe a sigh of relief as you read, knowing that you are not alone in experiencing what you are in this moment.

PREFACE

$\mathcal{E}$ ven though the main topic of this book is depression, I also talk about trauma and the PTSD diagnosis that usually follows. Obviously, if you have depression, it doesn't automatically mean that you also have PTSD, but, in my personal experience, those who have opened up to me about experiencing depression have also had some kind of traumatic experience that is triggered on a regular basis.

In order to save myself from continually repeating, "In my experience," or "This is EXPRESSLY MY OPINION," or "THIS IS NOT SCIENTIFICALLY PROVEN," I'd like to take this moment to say this entire book is comprised of my thoughts. Thoughts do not equal facts; only circumstances equal facts. What's the difference between a thought and a circumstance? I'm so glad you asked. A circumstance is something that can be proven in the court of law, such as "This man is eating cereal." (And now I want Lucky Charms. Great.)

Everything else is a thought. If it is still a wee-bit fuzzy, a circumstance is something that can be agreed upon by every rational person. Still confused? That's okay; this will hopefully become clearer as we move forward. "Hopefully" is the key word there because, who knows, you could finish this book and be hopelessly and utterly befuddled, for which I prescribe a big bowl of fresh fruit inside a nest of blankets and pillows. I believe all problems in this world can be solved with fruit and a nest of blankets, but, for some odd reason, society frowns upon presidents conducting meetings inside a blanket fort. Weird. Anyway, now that I declared myself totally incompetent to chat about the scientific workings of depression, I'm sure you just can't wait to hear my thoughts about the scientific workings of depression. Onward and upward!

My story

Please keep in mind: I am writing to myself as much as to you. I've had depression for about as long as I can remember. I attempted suicide in college, stayed in a mental hospital for several days (which caused some trauma all on its own), and then again was on the brink of hurting myself severely in 2022, (As this book was written very soon after, I clearly haven't been magically healed. I'm still processing and working and healing!)

My brother died when I was 8, and the aftermath that ensued with my family started my depression off with a bang. I was raped when I was 20, and then again when I was 25. Throughout my life, sexual harassment and minor assault have been common, further compounding my PTSD. As we will get into later, I worked in South Sudan for a while and, with the way women are treated there, it made it even worse.

With everything that I experienced, my depression grew worse. Sometimes, my depression felt warranted due to what was happening around me; at other times, I have been in the middle of a fantastic day and all I want to do is go home, curl up in a ball, and stare at the wall until my mind allows me to drift off into the sweet bliss of sleep. In 2022 my physical body decided to match the same level of functionality as my mentally-ill brain. Apparently, my body had enough of whatever it decided it had enough and broke down. I have never been in so much pain, daily, for months.

This didn't help my cause in trying to heal my brain. I have had multiple days over the past year where I exist in a state of so much pain that I cannot move. I just sit and breathe through the pain, never knowing if, or when, it will stop. Sometimes, it comes in waves and I get a reprieve every few hours. Sometimes, it doesn't stop for a few days. And if you too are in constant pain, you know the darkness that envelops you from your mental pain seems darker and denser now that physical pain has joined it. It seems to forcefully push those "no one cares if you would just disappear" thoughts to the forefront of your brain and focus on them as if a searchlight is shining brightly on those thoughts.

It took me a while (and Eye Movement Desensitization and Reprocessing therapy) to realize that a lot of the decisions I have made, and my depression, were a trauma response to my PTSD. I wish I could have written this book stating I am completely healed from depression and trauma, but that simply isn't true, and I will most likely have to deal with this for the rest of my life. But, I don't look at that statement with discouragement or anxiety. It's a part of my life and I can either choose to be angry about it, or I can look at myself with acceptance and compassion. I choose compassion. I share these things with you because I know that sometimes we don't know why we do the things we do. Looking at our trauma in a compassionate way enables us to understand our past and show compassion to that version of ourselves.

And guess what. Since I am not at the finish line for this, we are taking this journey together. You are not alone. My physical pain is here to stay for now, along with the mental pain. I'm still in the middle of this with you, running or walking (or crawling) on this journey.

As I share my story, and the tools I've used to create compassion and space for myself, I'm hoping you will be able to do the same. At first glance, depression and PTSD may not seem related, but, if you look closer, you'll see they both have a common need to build a relationship with ourselves and learn to trust and love what we need in that moment. We will be diving into this a lot for the duration of this book, but keep this in mind as we move forward. For both of these diagnoses, our reactions start with ourselves. Specifically, how we trust and treat ourselves. As we go about our daily lives, the triggers we experience can happen when we least expect it and I want to show you how we can process those triggers with compassion.

Who Am I Trying to Reach?

So, now you know I am not writing this book as though I am the Great and Magnificent Oz, who knows all and wants to help you poor peasants now that I am an expert at handling depression episodes and PTSD triggers. I am a human woman trying to figure this out myself, but I'm hoping it will help at least one other person to know you are not alone. As much as I would love this book to help others navigate depression and just cure them instantly, I can't wave a magic wand and make that wish come to fruition. (Shout out to the Harry Potter series for making me wish Hogwarts was real. Yes, I am one of THOSE nerds. More later.) When I first thought of the idea to write a book, my original goal was: I must help others. But it isn't possible to make it so; therefore, I altered my goal. At the very least, my hope is that this book can help you provide space and compassion for yourself.

Even if this book doesn't help anyone else, it still helps me, myself, and I. Since this book is filled with necessary reminders for me, it keeps my mind focused on the truth instead of the oh-so-enticing and fantastically "realistic" lies. I do hope it will at least help some to know they are not alone in figuring all of this out, nor are they broken. Hopefully this book will help you, my friend, to find some peace with the diagnosis of depression or PTSD, and applying that peace to your life, regardless of whether the diagnosis is yours or a loved one's. You know, help enable people to actually live instead of just trying to survive until bedtime when sleeping pills can be taken and the world forgotten for a blissful few hours. Unless, like me, PTSD comes knocking on your door with night terrors and reliving trauma. (THANKS A LOT PTSD!) At the very least, maybe this book will make you think that you aren't the wackiest wackadoo that ever lived. Success!

One final note

Know that you don't have to figure out any of this all at once. You've got all the time in the world and you WILL figure it out. Yes, yes, I know. We all want to figure this out RIGHT NOW, becoming impatient since all we want is to enjoy this life and, on our most ambitious days, make a difference to those around us. We really do have time. We've totally got this. All of this to say, you are in good company. Now that we have all of that out of the way, let's get into it!

Chapter 1

DEPRESSION, GOTTA LOVE IT

What phrase or feeling comes to mind when you think of the word "depression?" For me, it feels as if I'm trying to go about my daily life, but my brain and body are covered in molasses. I like to call this phenomenon "Molassified." As in, "Oh no, I've been molassified!"

PSA: I will be referring to words that aren't actually words for the remainder of this book. I mean, that's what our imagination is for, right? To find a word that can truly describe what you think, even if that word isn't listed in the dictionary. With that disclaimer, you've been sufficiently warned. Let's get back into it.

Molassified feels like shame and "not being enough" and constantly oscillating between striving for something more and lying in bed, staring at the wall, too tired to even sleep. You're just existing in the moment and not in a good way. But there's got to be more to life, right? In that moment, it doesn't feel like it. All that is going through your head is how tiring it would be to sit up, get out of bed, and conduct "normal" activities that others seem to do effortlessly. And you wonder, how do they do that? Where can I get that magic potion that makes it easy to take a shower or brush my hair?

Because of this, I've gone through days or even weeks of literally talking myself through everything and checking it off a list to keep myself sane and moving.

Wake up? Crushed that goal!
Put feet on the floor? Nailed it!
Stand up? Done and done!
Walk to the back door to let the dog out? Man,
I've accomplished so much already!

And, yes, it's tiring. Yes, it's challenging. And that's okay. Sure, we could choose to beat ourselves up and pour condemnation and judgment on top of our depression sundae. But, what if we didn't? What if we chose compassion and understanding? When we switch our reaction to our struggles, life becomes softer, kinder, and gentler. It becomes okay to only accomplish "a little" some days. And we can celebrate that. We got out of bed! We put on clean clothes! We fed ourselves and our fur babies and/or children. (My husband insists on calling them skin babies when fur babies are brought up in the same sentence. I feel like this is grounds for divorce. That and liking mayo. But, I digress.) And these "little" celebrations begin to snowball. And then some days are wonderful, some days you are excited about doing things. And then, at times, your brain slides back into the comfortable rut, the way your neuropathways have practiced for years and your brain is so good at choosing the easy way.

It's easier to be sad. It's easier to eat food to numb pain, or have sex to distract with that momentary pleasure, or drink until our body says we have alcohol poisoning. It's all normal. It really is. Nothing is wrong with you. Your brain is always trying to protect you, keep you from feeling pain. And, ironically, when your brain tries to protect you in the ways it has been trained, it causes negative consequences instead. But, you don't have to change. You really don't. If that's how you want to live your life, that is your choice to live exactly how you are living at this moment. I know this is weird and even sounds like a contradictory idea at first. I'm sure some people have stopped reading because they disagree and that is totally fine. To be clear, I am not condoning alcohol poisoning, binge eating, or unhealthy behaviors; I don't think they are the way we can fully and wholeheartedly enjoy our lives. But, humor me for a second and read on. Yes, it is your choice to continue living how you are living. When I first heard this thought, I was completely against it and resisted exploring this idea. After all, you "should" change, right? You "shouldn't" be doing unhealthy things in your life. But I invite you to consider this: when has someone ever made a permanent change in their life because they were pressured into it by themselves or others using a list of "shoulds"?

"But, Jen," you say, "what about people who were doing drugs, or drinking to black out, and people told them they should change, that they "had" to change, so they did?" Sure, some people say they overdosed one too many times and they "had" to change. But they still CHOSE to change. That is an extremely important distinction. It puts you back in the driver's seat. You are no longer a victim, allowing whatever to happen to you whenever it happens. You have power, you have agency. So, you can choose to keep going the way you are or you can choose to try something else. It's still your choice. You always have a choice. If you have depression and are reading this book, I'm going to take a stab in the dark and say you don't like living like this, and maybe have tried to change but have become discouraged.

I understand feeling discouraged if the first, or second, or fourteenth thing doesn't work at all, or does work but not long

3

term. It's fascinating (or, being completely honest, DUMB) when things that help some days do absolutely nothing on other days, which means you need to find another option to get yourself going. Or when things that help others and that they swear it's the only way they can get out of bed, make it worse for you. And you know what? That's okay too. Every human is different; think of all the likes and interests on which humans differ. Of course, one thing is not going to work for everyone. Our brains are funny and so cool like that. I will be going through several different ways that help me in order to perhaps help you get the ol' noodle turning for some ideas of your own. But if those don't work, it does not mean anything bad about you or your brain. It means that you can tweak the suggestions I give you, or discard them entirely and try something wholly different. Someone gave me this thought and I absolutely love it: trying new ways of thinking about things or doing things is like trying on different hats. You don't get mad at yourself because the hat doesn't work, you just take it off and try on another one. Of course, you can be frustrated and discouraged and sad that it didn't work, but you can feel that way and still keep moving forward. Negative emotion doesn't mean you're failing or moving backward or stagnate; it means you are human. And doing a fantastic job at being human! So, if you've experienced an emotion that you don't enjoy today, YAY! You're not a robot; you're human! Celebration time!

Okay, maybe you aren't ready for a celebration. Totally fine. That option is available whenever you'd like to try it.

Regardless if you choose to keep trying to change and get better, or if you choose to keep living the way you are living, other people will have opinions on who we are right now and what choice we made. We all have to deal with others' opinions of us, which sometimes correspond with what our own brains are saying to us. I'd love for you to join me in the next chapter as we discuss this further and get to the root of why those comments hurt so much.

Chapter 2

PEEPS BE PEEPIN'

My husband has a phrase that he will say when someone does something mean or annoying like cut him off in traffic or say something hurtful: "Peeps be peepin'!"

As silly as that sounds, maybe that's what we need to provide some levity to a situation or put some space between the anger and hurt so we can process it in a healthy way. People (aka peeps) are always going to be doing and saying things (aka peepin') that we choose to allow to irritate us, annoy us, or hurt us.

Peepin' from those who don't accept you

One reason we feel irritated, annoyed, or hurt is we give others power to hurt us because we desire to fit in and be accepted. You know the saying, "I just want to be different, just like everyone else"? No? Well now you have. You are so welcome. Well, it's true. We simultaneously want to be unique, and special, and stand out in the crowd so people acknowledge and envy us, and yet also blend in with everyone so we are loved and accepted and not isolated. Crazy how that works, huh? This isn't the first time, and most certainly won't be the last, I mention how hilariously awful our brains can be in the name of protecting us and keeping us alive. That's when you can call your brain a silly pickle because that's exactly how it's acting. Or, you can choose whatever vegetable you think is the silliest. I just happen to think it's a pickle. I mean, you've never met someone being serious while holding a pickle, have you? It's universally impossible. Try it, I dare you. Didn't think you would read about pickles in a depression book, did ya? Well, surprise! Much like depression, I don't leave anything out. I encompass all topics from pickles, to Harry Potter, to piles of cuddly little kittens (or puppies for those who have not evolved to liking cats yet—aka peasants).

Anyway, back to our regularly scheduled program. It's a universal truth that our brains tell us we need to be accepted and always fit in to society. Our need to be accepted often stops us from being our unique and genuine selves; and that is a tragedy. My husband and I once did a spur-of-the-moment water-aerobics dance duet to The Greatest Showman in the middle of a pool at a hotel in Hawaii while singing at the top of our lungs. I, unfortunately, did not record it myself. However, I'm sure we are on someone's Instagram for a good laugh. Or jealously wanting to be like us. Or both. Either way, total success. I love providing joy to others, especially when it's at my own expense. I'll be honest, I do a lot of weird things that "typical" women in their 30s don't do. But, then again, what is typical? What is normal? Why wouldn't we want to do whatever we want, regardless of how utterly ridiculous we appear to others? All that's stopping us is pride. Who needs that, right?

I should start a movement: NO PRIDE. Although, now that I write that, I feel like that could be take a different way than intended, especially given the fact that I am a straight woman. But, letting go of our pride brings us right back to the notion that we can't control what others think. And isn't that awesome? If I could control someone's thoughts about me, that means they could control my thoughts, too. I wouldn't want someone to be able to do that.

Other's opinions, and why they matter to us, is always a super fun subject. It's the dichotomy between the desire for complete independence and wanting to be included in every invitation. We make plans for the weekend and, when the time comes, we drag our feet to actually attend, yet we would be very hurt if we weren't invited. Or, we feel left out when we hear about a party or trip that we weren't asked to attend. But, if we actually stop to think about if we want to go, or if we even like the people with whom we would be spending time, we DON'T EVEN WANT TO GO. Why do we do this? Why is this our gut reaction? Great question. It deserves an answer. Maybe you want to know that people think of you, specifically. They want <u>you</u> there. You are <u>wanted</u>. The pull behind that thought is so powerful. Of course, you want to feel wanted. Think about what it was like back in the caveman days. We had to fit in because we needed to stay safe. If we were considered "too different," we would be kicked out and have to fend for ourselves. If you weren't included in things, you would most likely die. But now, in this century, that is no longer true. I invite you to consider this: What if it's okay that people don't include you in everything? What if, GOD FORBID, not everyone likes you and that doesn't mean there is anything wrong with you?

A comment that perfectly illustrates this point is one that I heard on the podcast "Better than Happy" by Jody Moore. (If you haven't heard of it, and you're a person and a podcast kind of peep, give her a listen. Mind will be blown. Guaranteed.)

Side note: I never thought I would be the type of person that would listen to podcasts on a daily basis…is this adulting??

Back to the topic at hand, Jody Moore everyone!

She said, "You could be the ripest, juiciest peach in the world, but not everyone likes peaches."

Simple as that. You could be absolutely perfect. Wear the cutest clothes, be the perfect size, say the right thing at the right time, and be charming and witty and good looking and someone STILL won't like you. No matter how hard you try, you will not be liked by 100% of the people with whom you come into contact.

Peepin' from those who do accept you

Even the people who do like you can still hurt you. When you have a mental illness, one thing many peeps love to do is give unsolicited advice and opinions to those who are struggling with mental health. Remember that list of "shoulds" that people have for you? Many times, they list out those "shoulds" and fully believe that if you would only complete their list, then you would be magically cured!

Let's be honest, it will be constant. Even though these peeps might be saying these things because they honestly care and they think they have all the answers, most of the time it is so incredibly discouraging because they are echoing the thoughts (lies) in your head that you're not enough. And believe me, I've had conversations like that with family and people I thought were close friends. It's never a fun time. You feel as though you're trying the best you can and trying to be honest with those around you, but they don't understand and choose not to try to understand. When someone close to you repeatedly says you should get off your medications, it hurts. When someone gives you a list of everything they believe you've done wrong with no way to try to repair the relationship, it hurts. Unspoken expectations always seem to be the death of a relationship. All you want to do is to have them accept you; to listen—actually listen—to you and try to understand. Sometimes they don't understand. But, you know what? That isn't the end. You and I have the choice to choose boundaries, to choose to whom we speak. We can put ourselves back in that driver's seat instead of passively sitting in the passenger's seat and allowing life to happen to us.

Depression loves to whisper all kinds of lies that sound so true and legitimate. And those lies gain even more traction when they start to come from the mouths of friends and family. Sometimes, that's literally the worst thing that can happen. Everything you think is "true" (those pesky lies again) seems to be "proven" by someone who is supposed to care for you and love and accept you. In reality, sometimes they don't understand when you open up to them, and that non-understanding turns to hurtful words that just so happen to be the exact same things your brain has been whispering to you. That's why it hurts so much: you think, or at least a part of you thinks, it's true. That's why any sentence hurts, right? Because a part of you believes it. If someone told me I had blonde hair or three noses, I would laugh and think how strange of a conversation this is and how they are absolutely wrong, because it is blatantly not true. But when lies that you may be able to recognize as lies in your head come out of others' mouths, they can suddenly turn into truth and condemnation. Your brain will then keep churning those thoughts over again in your mind like a washing machine or a cow chewing cud, unconsciously filing it away in the cabinet of proof that you're not enough.

Peepin' from yourself:

Depression is so trixy, isn't it? It turns things you don't do into a statement of "you're not enough." As crazy as it may sound, sometimes you are the one doing the peepin'. It's so easy to collect evidence for that thought; that filing cabinet becomes the biggest you have in your brain if you let it. But you don't have to keep collecting for that particular cabinet. You can start another filing cabinet. Find evidence that you ARE enough and start filing those away. Make it a goal to see if you can get that filing cabinet bigger than the first.

Will that be easy peasy lemon squeezy? Maybe, maybe not. If your brain is anything like mine (and for your sake, I really hope not), then it's not going to be as easy as flipping a switch. Let's ponder why for a moment. For years, you've been thinking "I'm not enough." Your brain has found that evidence because that's what it's looking for. That "NOT ENOUGH" cabinet has grown. So now, when you look in the mirror, for example (which I'm pretty sure we all do at least once a day), you automatically think, "I don't look good." And then, that higher brain kicks in and tries to redirect to "No, we don't think that way anymore. We don't demean ourselves."

But then, thanks to the years of filing, your brain pipes in with, "Wait! Of COURSE, we don't look good. Look at all this evidence we've collected! We don't want that to go to waste! It's easy to pull out some evidence about this. What about that one time 10 years ago that we can use? That's a doozy. Let's use that. It would take too much brain power and effort to think of something that goes against that evidence. So, let's just stick with the thought that you don't look good."

Sounds like a whiny little kiddo who doesn't want to do a chore, huh? But that makes complete sense. Our brain's job is to do as little work as possible. Because of this, our brain is like a little toddler throwing a tantrum when we are trying to redefine the way we have been thinking about ourselves for years. Now, we don't need to be mad at the toddler; they are doing what they have always done. They don't know any better, YET.

We can always redirect back to the thought that we don't do that anymore. Follow it up with evidence that we do, in fact, look good. Pick something specific. Your eyes? Your eyebrows? Your nose? The fact that your elbows bend correctly? And that step, little though it may seem, puts a new piece of evidence in that new filing cabinet. And then the next time in the mirror, when your brain tries to pipe in again with that old evidence, you can pull up the new filing cabinet. Of course, this will take time, but it's worth it. You can get in plenty of practice because mirrors are pretty common in this world, unless you're in a compound in South Sudan and then not so much. But remember, "Peeps will always be peepin'" and sometimes that peep is you. You can choose to redirect all those lovely little thoughts from your peep. My point is, you can choose which filing cabinet you are going to fill when you look in a mirror. What kind of evidence do you want to find? That is what your brain will look for and provide.

Keep filling up your cabinet with evidence for why you are enough, reminding yourself that "peeps be peepin'" and not everyone will like the juicy peach that you are. I won't lie to you, it is tough. Even if you logically know that people will say hurtful things that you just have to ignore, and that not everyone will like you, it can still be discouraging. No one likes to feel like others don't like them. But, remember the file cabinet and the ability to choose? You could choose to be discouraged that so-and-so doesn't like you, OR you could focus on finding the people that click WITH YOU, with your genuine, authentic self: the person you want to be, the person you want to show up as, and not someone you think the other person wants you to be. You could find the people that make you better, that make you want to be better. It's freeing to think about, right? Since you don't have to strive for an impossible and unattainable goal, it opens your heart and soul to the most meaningful relationships you can make with people that are truly YOUR PEOPLE. You end up building relationships that are genuine, lasting, and built on trust. And that's what humans seek, that's what we desire in this life. We long for connection, which can be difficult to navigate with mental illness as we'll see in the next chapter.

Chapter 3

MENTAL ILLNESS AND RELATIONSHIPS

Since I'm an introvert, I thought I would be totally fine during the isolation stay-at-home order in 2020 for the COVID pandemic. Did I think it would be paradise that I wouldn't have to see anybody? Yep, you bet your bottom dollar. Did that happen? Yes... for about 2 months. And then I started to become a bit Looney Tunes. I had just moved to Arlington, VA a few months before the pandemic, so I had no community, no friends, no significant other, and no roommates except my dog. So, really, the only human interaction I had for a while was passing masked-up humans in a grocery store or on the street when I would walk my dog. It was not fun, even for an extremely introverted introvert. All of this to say, we all need some form of human connection. It's how we are wired. I need people; I always have. I just didn't need the wrong type of people.

One of the biggest realizations that helped me was the knowledge that I didn't have to continue to chase friendships with people that weren't MY PEOPLE. What do I mean by that? Thanks for asking! When I say MY PEOPLE, I mean the people that respect me, seek to understand me, seek to love me, and are honest with me in a loving way. Or, maybe as L.M. Montgomery calls them, "Kindred spirits." Those are people to hold onto and cherish. People who are willing to be there, even when they didn't know what to say or didn't understand the struggle. Or, people who are willing to have an awkward conversation about hurts and still want to hear from you. They want to know YOU. All of you. Not the mask you think you need to put on so you don't lose relationships. It's such a huge game changer.

And if you're sitting there thinking that you have no desire to have friends, ask yourself why. Check in with yourself. What do you think might happen? Reaching out to people for friendship and connection might seem scary or vulnerable; that's okay. Of course you're feeling like that. We could get hurt. (There goes that silly pickle of a brain again.) But, what if we do reach out and it becomes a meaningful friendship; the kind of friendship where, even when you don't see each other for years, it's as if no time has passed when you do meet up? Those are relationships worth pursuing. Some of the friendships I was most afraid to start have been the best ones of my life. What do you think? Do you think you might like to try that? If you're not ready, totally fine. You don't have to do anything with my offers, remember? Just an invitation to think about the possibility of trying.

But, when you are ready, know that you will find your people. It may be a struggle, but you can do it. So, let's talk about how to navigate relationships when you have a mental illness.

Finding your people

Sometimes when you have depression, PTSD, or any other mental illness, the words in your head get stuck between your brain and your tongue and it takes some time to release the paralysis. So, you need relationships with people who seek to understand; if they don't understand, they wait in silence and compassion. Those people who seek to understand are okay with just being there until you are able to form the words to speak what's on your mind. They don't force you to speak, guilt you into speaking, or shame you by telling you that if you actually love them you would speak. Instead, they understand that sometimes the words aren't there yet. Because they have compassion, they're okay with you being upset and scared and not knowing why you're upset and scared.

They fully accept everything about you and love you for your strength and perseverance to keep going, even when everything in your head is screaming to just give up. This takes so many fun forms (wall staring, for instance). Becoming so zoned-out and discouraged and overwhelmed with despair that staring at a wall seems like a perfect use of your time. I could get a gold medal in the category of wall staring; or staring at my keyboard. I'm pretty darn good at that, too. And in those moments, suicidal thoughts are usually hopping around too, poking their heads in the door, asking if it's their turn to chime in. It's their time to shine!

My best friend (yes, even 30-year olds can have best friends), Adrienne, was the first person who showed me this kind of compassion. Every time I shared something that, in my mind, would have made anyone run away, screaming for a restoration of sanity, she accepted it. She accepted me. All. Of. Me. Not just the pretty, flowery parts. But, the suicidal thoughts, the night terrors, and the raging against the gender of men as a whole; well, more specifically, straight men. She never told me I shouldn't feel the way I do or that I should just pray more to God or that taking depression meds were of the devil. She encouraged me that everything I'm experiencing is normal and does make complete sense. And that makes all the difference in the world. It gives you that sensation of tears welling up at someone's kindness and acceptance.

Fun fact: Kindness makes me cry. Anyone else? Just me? Either way, I'm fine with it. It's one of the things that gets the waterworks flowing, people being kind and doing things for others. And not doing them out of obligation, or people pleasing, or because they are expecting something in return. It's a gift. In experiencing that kind of agape love from another person, it enabled me to believe that it was possible to experience that from a significant other.

I didn't know this was possible in a significant other until my relationship with my now-husband. I had grown up in a household where it was frowned upon to be mad, or sad, or any emotion that is classified as negative in our society. I don't say this maliciously. Given that they had pretty terrible childhoods themselves, and had their own stuff to process, my parents did the best they could. But, the way I was raised did not work for my brain. I need to allow myself to be mad or sad to enable me to process through and choose what emotion I want to feel about that particular circumstance.

To those who have a loved one that struggles with mental illness

If you're a parent who has a child struggling with depression, and you are now berating yourself because you feel you didn't give your child the relationship they needed, and should have done this or that, you don't have to do that anymore. Yes, you can apologize to them if you want, but then you can choose to leave the past in the past. You can choose to take the lessons you've learned and apply them to your children now (adults or children), providing grace, compassion, and humility when you do mess up.

A friend of mine came up with this analogy to explain living in the present and not the past. Think of your life as several train tracks running in parallel. One is childhood, one is middle school, one is high school, and so on, with other train tracks being continuing stages of your life. You're not on that original childhood track anymore. You're on this current track, today's track, whatever stage in life that may be. You have different tools, options, and wisdom now than you did earlier in the relationship with a loved one who struggles with mental illness. You can choose to continue on today's track. That's how you can move forward. You don't have to hop backwards to the past with the old you and lack of knowledge or tools. Will your children or friends bring up your mistakes? Maybe. But, it is still your choice to choose your next step. What will you choose to do in that moment?

> Choose to be angry at them for being hurt?
> Choose to insist you never did that thing?
> Or, choose to let them have their anger, and
> remind yourself that you still love yourself, with
> allllll your stuff and not just the nice stuff?

I mean, it would be great if we never hurt anyone. Life would be so easy. But, it wouldn't be life. Life and relationships are messy. Yeah, yeah, that's what everyone says, right? Well, it might be a thought that helps. Nothing has gone wrong when relationships are messy or miscommunications are had. Believe me, I would love to be perfect (you know, the whole robot thing), but that just isn't possible in this life. What if we are okay with accepting that we have hurt the other person, apologizing to them, and moving on? You can choose to think that you know better having learned that lesson, and now you can use that information, that knowledge, to continually improve and treat others in a better way. It's up to you. How do you want to show up for yourself and for those around you?

When others hurt you or you hurt them

When you have hurt someone, it is important to have compassion for both yourself and the other person. Ironically, having compassion for yourself and for the one you hurt enables you to move forward and improve, instead of resisting and putting up walls, which leave you stagnant in your life and wallowing in your past. But, I do understand the appeal. I'll be the first to admit that wallowing is easy. It deceptively seems as though it's more helpful to keep your booty firmly planted in victim or self-shaming mode. And I get that change seems scary, intimidating, and not worth it.

This also works the other way. If you struggle with mental illness and someone hurts you, you have the choice to find compassion. You can be hurt and compassionate at the same time. Are you a little skeptical? I get it. I've been there and still experience occasional bouts of HOW IN THE WORLD AM I SUPPOSED TO BE HURT AND COMPASSIONATE AT THE SAME TIME??

> **Note:** When your brain asks a question, *always* answer it. There's a reason why your brain is asking; it really wants an answer. That's how our brains work. Don't just stop at the question. Answering can lead you to a wonderful, understanding, and compassionate place.

So, how do we do this? How are we able to be hurt and also feel compassion at the same time? We could start with curiosity about the other person. (Stay with me here.) By all means, if you want to stay in hurt, you can. It is your choice. When you're ready, you have the option of wondering why they did the things they did or said the things they said. It can also be known as "putting yourself in their shoes," but, for some reason, that phrase doesn't always land with my brain. So, sometimes I take off that "thought hat" and try a different thought, like the one below:

> *"Ok, Lucy really hurt me. I know she is hurt too. I know that people always have a reason for things they do. Maybe she was embarrassed, or filled with shame, and that is why she lied. I can understand that. Sometimes my shame tempts me to lie or hide. Maybe it's a reflex reaction to not get in trouble. Maybe she's afraid that I will leave the friendship if she tells me the truth."*

You can pick any of those reasons. And, you know what? Those might not be the reasons. We are trying to see it from their perspective, but we will not really know until we are able to read minds. (If anyone has perfected this technology, contact me ASAP.) But, picking one of these options enables us to have compassion. It enables us to love Lucy, forgive, and move forward.

Sometimes leaving is the answer

Now, just because you forgive someone doesn't mean you need to keep the relationship. If you're in an abusive relationship, get the heck out of Dodge! If you have a friend continually lying to you, and trust is important to you, it doesn't mean you close your eyes to the lies and just continue on in the relationship. You can love her and love YOU at the same time. Remember, you can choose your own people. You don't NEED to stay in any relationship. Realizing that I could do that was mind blowing. I didn't have to be around people that weren't kind to me or didn't respect me.

A concept that I absolutely hate, and am still getting used to, is that some friendships are for a season. Sometimes that season is for decades; sometimes that season is for a few months. I used to think that loyalty was the be-all and end-all in relationships. At the risk of accidentally condoning adultery, loyalty is not always the right answer. A few more people have probably stopped reading; maybe I'll have at least one person who finished this book; or, it might just be my poor editor.

Loyalty is, of course, a great trait in a relationship, but if the friendship is going against your values or your morality, it may be time to say goodbye. That actually reminds me of an interview question. They asked me what the most important trait was: perseverance, loyalty, or integrity. It's integrity, right? You can be loyal to a fault (which I have been for most of my life; the "to a fault" part, but you really do come crashing down from that), but, if it's going against your integrity, you are going against yourself.

If having integrity means ending the relationship and not being loyal to it, then pick integrity and leave. It doesn't have to be a hateful goodbye, or you making a big deal about it, like saying, "I WILL CUT YOU OUT OF MY LIFE." (It reminds me of the people who decide to unfollow others on Instagram and announce it in the comments.) You can be honest about your decisions if they ask you, or if you don't want to ghost them without being unkind. Once again, you can love them, and love you, and still decide to say goodbye, as painful as that would be.

What is the healthiest choice for you? What do you want? Like, actually want? If you want to stay, then stay. If you want to leave, then leave. And yes, I am aware it is incredibly easy for me to sit here and write this, but oh-so challenging to actually put into action. But please know, O reader of mine, that I am going through this situation as I write this book. So, I am most definitely talking to myself as much as to you. This season of letting this particular friendship go might last for a few months, a year, or longer. But, in this moment, my healthiest choice is to say goodbye for now. It hurts. It really hurts. Like many introverts, I don't make friends easily; therefore, when I make a friend, they are a friend that I anticipate keeping for the rest of my life. (Shout out to loyalty to a fault! A blessing and a curse.) The pain I feel right now is akin to the pain of going through a breakup. But I know, for me, in this moment, it is the right thing.

The truth about relationships

Relationships are hard; they are messy. But, when you have a relationship you want—like actually want—then stay and work through the mess. People you love will hurt you, and you will hurt people you love. But, even with those emotions, there's hope, freedom, joy, and peace. It's there, I promise. And, yes, it may be overwhelming when you are in a vulnerable enough place to allow someone to see all of you, the grossness you feel and loathing you may have for yourself. But it can also be very beautiful to be yourself and be fully accepted for every part of you—Adrienne and my husband have shown me that.

I hope you have an Adrienne or a significant other like my husband, but, if you don't, you always have the option of starting that relationship with yourself. Being okay with ALL OF YOU. That whole "being a human" shenanigan, remember?

Now, I know it may sound a little "woo-woo" to you, and that's valid. It sounded a bit hippy-dippy-roll-your-eyes to me when I first decided to look into this idea. I absolutely did not think this was going to work. I mean, the whole "get in touch with yourself" and "your most important relationship is with you, yourself, and you" concept is one of those things you imagine seeing on the wall, along with the "Live, Laugh, Love" and "Dance Like No One Is Watching." But, it really is the place to start.

You can't truly connect with others without diving into the relationship with yourself first. It's the root. Think about it. It connects with the idea that "hurt people hurt people." When have you ever heard of a person being cruel and hateful to someone and they are a totally whole soul who is acting from a place of love? That would be ridiculous. It wouldn't make sense. It's laughable. If you can be curious and dig into your relationship with yourself, it has the ripple effect of spreading to your other relationships. Mind you, this doesn't mean we are going to jump into the judgement pool. We aren't going crazy berating ourselves for the things we aren't doing correctly. We've already got depression pounding that into us; we don't need any more, just like we don't need people who don't want to understand what's going on in our heads.

Let's make a pact with ourselves that we are going to treat ourselves like a really close friend who is struggling. If our close friend came to us and was upset about something they did or didn't do, we wouldn't slap them across the face and then rub their faces in their mistakes, right? If we wouldn't do that to someone we love, why we would do that ourselves? And, yes, it is so easy to dump on ourselves, especially when depression comes knocking. But, you have another choice. You do. It's always there for you to access if you want to access it.

I want you to ask yourself this:

Do you like who you are right now?
Do you want to keep on doing what you are doing,
or would you like to live a different way?
Do you like how you are showing up for yourself?

If the answer is yes, then that's okay. If the answer is no, that's okay too. (Remember, no judgement! Do a swap-a-roo for curiosity instead of judgement.) You can choose to change.

You have the option to take steps that allow you show up in a healthy way.

If you don't have someone who can help you do that, and you feel like therapy is not the right step right now, contact me on my website, *http://www.staringatwalls.com*. In this space, you have the opportunity to vent, ask for advice, or just exist with some beautiful music and calming scenery. I can hold some space for you and just exist with you in that moment of paralysis. I can hold space for you until you can hold space for yourself. Once you are able to hold space for yourself, you'll be able to start loving yourself and others at the same time consistently, creating a life that you want to live for yourself. When you're ready to learn more, come join me in the next chapter to talk about the six-letter F-word.

Chapter 4

THE SIX-LETTER F-WORD

*L*et's talk about the six-letter F-word. Yep, I'm talking about good ol' FAMILY. And, yes, I had to count on my fingers to double check. May seem like something you would automatically know but, hey, since when do people actually count the number of letters in a word?

Did you check my math? I'm betting about 75% of you did, and I love it. This may seem like a strange chapter to put in the middle of a mental-health-focused book, and it might be. But, one thing I have learned is that family has quite a bit of impact on mental health. When dealing with mental health and family, you have to create boundaries and learn to love yourself and others at the same time. Yes, even for our family, we need to have boundaries for healthy, growing relationships. If we don't set up boundaries, if we allow our family's opinions to become part of our identity, we end up putting ourselves right back in that passenger's seat and allowing their emotions to influence us. Remember hearing about the thoughts that depression feeds our mind that we also hear from others? In my experience, it mostly comes from family. If we don't look into what we need and then seek to fulfill that need ourselves, we are going to start listening to those lies that we aren't enough, or whatever unhelpful things your brain/family is telling you.

I never thought I would be one of those people who had issues with their family. For years, I had told myself over and over again, ad nauseum, that my family was a great family, that my parents were great parents, that I had everything for which to be thankful, and nothing should be questioned. Nope, that's not exactly it. At the moment, I am processing through some family issues, so you all get to benefit (from actual helpful thoughts or just for mild amusement!).

Letting your parents expectations go

Maybe you are one of those lucky ducks that have a supportive family: parents that accept that you are an adult who doesn't live in their house anymore and makes their own decisions.

But, if you are an adult and your parental units/guardians are American, you most likely are in the same boat as me. Let's not beat around the bush like some other beat-around-the-bushers. Parents (or whoever raised you) have a hard time letting go. And, even more than that, all parents have plans and ideas of who their children will be, how they will act, who they will marry (aka expectations). Expectations can be such a slippery, dangerous slope like we discussed when it comes to other relationships. Some are spoken, some are unspoken. Those expectations start way before we are even born, they stay with us as children, and then as we grow up and move out of our parent's house, they still manage to follow us. I was going to say follow us like a lamb, but I was thinking something slimier and more disgusting like an eel, if eels followed people.

And, here's the thing: our parents are ALWAYS going to have expectations of us. And, yes, they will be disappointed or upset if we don't meet those expectations, but that's where that disappointment can stop. We have the choice to not take on that disappointment from our parents or whoever have their opinions of how we should live our life. Frankly, them being upset is NONE OF OUR BUSINESS; it isn't. And it has NOTHING to do with us. It's their choice to be upset with our choices and not our responsibility to make them feel better. They might think so, but that doesn't matter because it isn't true.

Honestly, maybe they need to be upset with us. When they are upset, they feel like they have a valid reason to be. We don't have to agree with them, and we don't have to take that negative emotion onto ourselves. It isn't our responsibility to make them feel better or to change their mind about our decisions that we make for our own lives. It is my life, your life, and they don't have a say in that.

But, maybe those niggling thoughts at the back of your mind are popping back up:

I need them to know that I am not an awful person.
I need them to move on.
I need them to protect me.
I need them to be kind to me and to love and accept me.

Do you? Do you need them? Or are you just exposing the parts in your life where you don't have your own back?

Are you telling yourself that you are not an awful person?
Are you moving on?
Are you protecting yourself?
Are you being kind to yourself and
loving and accepting yourself?

And even deeper into the realms of thought land:

How can I move on?
How can I protect myself?
How can I be kind to myself and love and accept myself?

Of course, our first step is acknowledging that pain, that sadness that we weren't accepted the way we should have been. But, when we are ready, we come back to the train tracks analogy; we aren't on that train track anymore. We weren't accepted back then, but we can accept ourselves now. We have those new tools, those new thoughts we can utilize. Our parents are no longer responsible for accepting us. What would it look like if we released that expectation? What if we changed our expectations of our parents to just a couple of humans trying to have a healthy relationship? How would you show up with that in mind?

Boundaries are your friend

I'm not saying this isn't difficult. After 31 years, I finally put some healthy boundaries in place with my parents and, lo and behold, they weren't exactly pleased. As of writing this, I haven't heard from them in almost three months. Three months may seem like a very short time to you, but to someone who talked to her parents on an almost daily basis, it is torture (pause for dramatic effect). I never thought my parents would refuse to speak to me. And over a request for boundaries at that. But, friends, here's the thing. When you request boundaries from someone who has never learned how to set and keep boundaries themselves, it sounds like an ultimatum. And then they create a story in their heads that this boundary-setting person (ahem, me) doesn't love them, wants to control them, and is being unkind, untruthful, and hurtful. They don't see that the BSP (see what I did there?) loves them and wants them in her life and that's why she is setting boundaries. If she didn't love them, she wouldn't care. She would be completely indifferent to the relationship and would be fine with cutting contact entirely.

And here's the thing about your parents, or whichever family member is being a silly pickle right now: You could stand in front of them, tap dancing and repeating your words until you're blue in the face, and they still wouldn't believe you because they have their story and they don't want to let that go. That would mean they might be wrong and, for them, that is incredibly scary. I mean, let's be real, it IS scary to question if you are actually in the wrong. Over the past few months, I've started to realize more and more that I have some tendencies that I hate. It was a right kick in the pants. But, I'm not casting judgement on myself. Am I embarrassed? You betcha. But, awareness really is that first step; that, and a plan to move forward to see how that can be changed so I can be the person I truly want to be. But, for those who aren't ready to take a good look at themselves, it is scary, and so it makes sense why our family members resist this so vehemently. They are going to believe whatever they want to believe. If they have stories that aren't true, it means they don't want to listen to the truth. They don't want to know the actual truth, they aren't curious or seeking to understand the situation. We know the story isn't true and, yet, it still hurts. We have people in our life who we love and with whom we want a good relationship and we can't make that relationship happen. We can't make them like us or want to talk to us or even attempt to reconcile and move forward. And I'm not talking about just sweeping things underneath the rug. That's something that will exacerbate the depression and anxiety. And man, it feels pretty awful. But, they've decided what the truth is in their mind and we can't control that.

We can, however, control how we act in the situation. We can control our boundaries. You can still love your family and choose to have no contact with them if they choose to disregard your boundaries. At this time, our parents/family member/ you fill in the blank, may not be capable of entertaining those boundaries or having that relationship. That doesn't mean we cave and go back to the way things were. They are not capable of having a relationship with us and we are not capable of going back to the way we were treated in that relationship without healthy boundaries. Unfortunately, if they choose to stick to their story, everything you say and do will be colored by that story. Hello worldview and perspective! Because of this, staying in contact won't be healthy for you.

My friend, I won't lie to you, this will feel pretty terrible sometimes. At these times, instead of life feeling 50/50, it may feel like 99/1, especially when depression is tagging along for the ride. But we've still got this. You can take all the time in the world you need to grieve that lack of relationship; it's a normal thing to grieve for the brokenness in relationships. In the words of Brené Brown, "If you didn't, you would be a sociopath."

So, invite that sadness in, feel the vibrations of those uncomfortable emotions in your body (we will get more into this later). When you're ready, you will always have the choice, the option, to move forward in accepting that this relationship is not the way you want it to be and decide who you want to be in this relationship.

Loving and being yourself

You get to control who you want to be. You can't control others' stories, but you can control how you think about them and how you choose to show up for yourself.

What does that look like for you?

How can you love others AND love yourself at the same time?

We can love ourselves and love them from a distance until they are capable of upholding the boundaries that have been set in place. We will be there whenever they are able and, until then, we can build relationships with others that are willing and able to listen to us and seek to understand how we are feeling.

What can you do to love others and yourself at the same time? The answer, like all things in this world, might change from day to day. But, that's where we can start. Remember, we aren't locking into one protocol or one answer for life. Life is fluid and we can look at that with frustration that nothing stays the same or we can observe it with a sense of fun and curiosity. Your needs today do not dictate your needs for tomorrow and that's a wonderful thing! You won't be the same every single day; remember, you aren't a robot! Let's embrace that humanity and that flexibility, accepting all of it. So, what do you want for today in those relationships you are thinking about right now?

The answer to that isn't something a friend, pastor, therapist, priest, shaman, or any Joe Schmoe on the street can decide for you. It may seem easier to ask anyone and everyone what you should do in a sticky situation, but that's not living for you. It's not you deciding who you want to be. It's living through other people until your life is a mish-mash of decisions from 50 different people. We don't want that because that isn't truly us. And this is coming from a girl who has only recently started asking myself what I actually want in this life.

I relied on pleasing everyone else around me, mostly my parents, for the decisions in life: my major, my college, where I decided to live, my career, my hobbies, my church, my schoolwork and many more things. In an effort to make my parents like me, almost none of my decisions were actually mine for years. I became this weird fake-mask person who had no idea who she actually was and what she truly wanted. I'm finally starting to live for me, the real me. The awesome me. That's what I want for you. I may never meet you, but you are awesome. You are. Look at you, reading this book, trying to learn things from a crazy loon, even when you are struggling with so much.

That's strength right there. That's courage. That's determination. You're still going, you're still trying and you're not giving up, even when your mind is doing allll sorts of mental gymnastics in an effort to persuade you otherwise.

Use that strength now to learn at least this one thing from this crazy loon: It is time to live life for yourself. It is time to set boundaries with your family and loved ones. And it is time to love yourself. We can acknowledge the uncomfortability of doing all that and still move forward. We don't have to immediately skip to sunshine and daises, unicorns, and frolicking happily in fields of clover to be loving life and improving ourselves. Each improvement is a small step. Later on, I will talk about the Depression Protocol. Start with one of those, do it every day for 30 days and make it a habit. I know it sounds so cliché to talk about that 1% growth, but we don't change all at once. That's not how we were made to be, and it would be unnatural if we did a complete 180-degree about-face of our lives. It's not sustainable. Let's practice that 1% and once we have a handle on that (let's be real, we are never going to be perfect, so let's shoot for 80%), move on to the next habit.

Some people will 110% not agree with that last statement and I would not have either a few years ago. But that black and white thinking, the all or nothing mantra, going balls-to-the-wall or laying on a couch 24/7 while eating bags of potato chips, leads to stagnation. Most of us can't just flip a switch. If you are one of those peeps, that is amazing and keep doing you! But, for kiddos like me, I need gradual change and grace for myself and saying that 80% is good enough. This enables me to keep going and keep pushing for high standards, but also be okay if I fall short. I can't punish myself into being a healthier, more accomplished, or kinder person. I already tried that and failed miserably. If you are anything like me, you used to punish yourself as well. We don't need to do that anymore. We've punished ourselves enough. Maybe it's time for a change. Maybe it takes kindness towards ourselves and those little steps that we take to build habits that build morning routines and a circle of people that we trust to support us, especially on our bad mental days. And maybe, just maybe, we can strive to help others when they need it.

Chapter 5

HELPING OTHERS (MAYBE)

A friend told me today that she was diagnosed with depression. As much as I hate that she is struggling with that, I'm glad she told me. Sometimes, in the midst of struggling yourself, the knowledge that someone else you know and care about is out there dealing with the same thing helps pull your mind out of the darkness into which it falls. By talking with her, I could get the focus off me. But that's me. It might not be the same for you.

You do not have to take on any more than you can handle right now. If someone comes to you with something, and your mental capacity is already tapped out, you have the choice to let them know that and ask to speak at a different time, or even have them send you an audio message that you can listen to when you do have more mental capacity. I realize that may not be a popular opinion (I'm getting the sneaking suspicion that there's a lot of those in this here book), but how will you be able to handle someone's stuff if you're already tapped out? And you know you best. I know it may seem harsh/selfish/enter any negative personality trait, but we don't lift others by pushing ourselves down.

When you do have mental capacity, you can always go back to that person and ask if they want to talk about it. When someone comes to you to talk, and your mental capacity is shot for the day, your brain needs to know it's okay to say, "Not right now." Going back to building that trust relationship between your body and brain, if your brain is telling you not right now, maybe we can honor that without guilt or shame. Let's accept where we are right now on this day. Once that processing happens, or you come back out of the depressive state, things start to seem more manageable. You have more space now to be the person you are at your core, the person who listens and supports their friend. Your friend may not understand and that's okay; it sounds like they have their own processing to do and we can allow them to do it.

If you do have capacity to listen to others and be able to support them, it enables another connection and more safe space for those who have a mental diagnosis. You know exactly what they are going through and you have the opportunity to show them they aren't broken. In today's world, mental illness has become more of a conversation and the stigma is less than it used to be, but it is still out there. I admit, writing this book is another way I am making peace with the fact that I have been diagnosed with depression and PTSD. So many people struggle with these things, but are still unwilling to speak openly and freely about it for fear of others' opinions. And I get that. To be honest, there are several people who I hope never know that I wrote this book. But, I know one thing: every time someone opens up, it makes another step towards a society and culture that understands the human condition and is okay with people sometimes going almost comatose in their bed for a few days. "Is okay" might be the wrong phrase. How about "a society who gives compassion freely to those who sometimes go almost comatose in their bed for a few days?"

All of these things are going to need little steps, taken one at a time. As awesome as it would be to flip the "perfect robot" switch, our change in lifestyle is going to take time and rewiring of those neuropathways. If you need the rest of your life to get yourself to a good place, that's okay. If you are partway in your healing journey and feel like you have space to help others, that's okay too. That was part of the reason I wrote this book. Even though I am not at the finish line of my depression race, I love the idea that maybe my struggle can help others. And not in a "misery loves company" kind of way, but it makes the days of talking myself through all the motions of a regular human being worth it. I've always wanted my life to mean something and this is my outlet, currently. When we know that someone else in the world is experiencing the same thing we are, it provides so much compassion and understanding. In turn, that person knows someone understands and it can make all the difference in the world.

Chapter 6

"SOMETIMES I WANT TO DIE" AND OTHER LOVELY THOUGHTS

I realize the title might sound dramatic, but for those that have depression and suicidal thoughts on a daily basis, thinking that we want to die is a thought that comes into our minds regularly. Can you acknowledge that sometimes it just pops into our heads for no reason? We can let that thought pop in, but it doesn't have to be as powerful as we think it is. Yes, on some bad mental days, it's a bit harder to allow ourselves to acknowledge, but what if we could practice another way to consider this thought?

One of my favorite ways is to put a humorous spin on it because, let's face it, those with mental illness tend to have a real dark sense of humor. Let's use that to our advantage. Let's think about the Dementors in Harry Potter for a minute. If you haven't read these books, what are you waiting for?? If you have, then you know what Dementors do. They swoop around with all their swoopiness to spread despair and sadness to people around them. When those thoughts come to mind, I've been practicing the thought, "Gosh, there are a lot of Dementors around today. That must be why I'm feeling so terrible." Sure, that may sound absolutely ridiculous, but is anything else helping? Sometimes mental illness needs a little ridiculousness to give it a swift kick in the rear. It helps to put that depression and those suicidal thoughts back in the passenger seat. You're the driver, remember? Those thoughts are along for the ride, and sometimes they are terrible passengers; trying to backseat drive, yelling at random intervals just for the sake of yelling, crunching celery super loudly when you're trying to hear the music. BUT. They are still passengers. They don't control you. You are still driving, you get to decide your next move, what direction you're going to take.

Finding what to live for

I want to want to live for me. Maybe you do too. But, as I write this, today is not one of those days. (See, told ya I still struggle with suicidal thoughts!) Today is one of those days where I want the pain, physical and mental, to end. I have a friend, a few years younger than myself, that is currently fighting Stage 4 cancer. For the second time. When I first heard this, I was angry and confused. I still continue to struggle with this on days like today. How can someone who wants to live, and wants many more years on this earth, have cancer while I, someone who has often had desires to die since I was in high school, can't seem to die. Why couldn't I be the one who has cancer? I wish I could take it from her; I wouldn't fight it. I wouldn't tell anyone. I would just let it take me home. Home to a place of no sin and no pain, only peace and joy.

So, today I'm choosing to live for my husband and for my dog. Even though everything inside me is urging me to just end it. Or to sit with my back against a wall and not move. But, instead, I choose to focus on the next thing and hope and pray that someday, I'll want to live for me. I hope that the idea of living for me will grow and take hold and become second nature. I hope and long for that day. But, today is not that day.

If you are in this same spot, who or what do you want to live for? Maybe you want to live to see tomorrow's amazing sunrise? Or sunset? Always a debate on which one is better. I tend toward the sunrise since the birds are louder, but maybe the sunset is your cup of tea. Maybe you want live for that little ball of fluff for whom you care and you know they would be so confused if you weren't there day after day. Maybe there's a new book or video game or movie coming out in a month. Of course, you've got to experience that! Find that reason, that purpose. It helps you get through those not-so-great days until you can grow that desire to live for yourself. And please, please: if/when you find yourself in a place like this, you have the option of calling a suicide hot line or calling a friend or something that can move your brain just a tick. That's all we need. Just a tick of motivation to get you through that depression session. Ha! Depression session. Sounds like something from that old game/ show Schoolhouse Rock ("Conjunction junction, what's your functionnnnnn").

Be done with punishing yourself

After you have decided to live and have found what you want to live for, consider the possibility of being done with punishing yourself. Can we make a pact right now? Can we make a pact that we are not going to punish ourselves anymore? Just because we have mental illness, or because we aren't perfect little robots, does not mean that we need to punish ourselves. We don't need to pick at our skin, bite our nails, pull out our eyebrows, cut, or eat until we feel sick. I know those actions are sometimes a release from the pain, but what if we invited that pain in and asked it to talk? (I feel myself losing some readers, but in all fairness, you did choose to read a book about mental illness written by a mentally-ill person.) Did you know you have that option? To check in with yourself and ask how you're feeling. Ask yourself why you are repeating these behaviors.

Are you punishing yourself?
Are you trying to avoid a painful situation?
Are you thinking that if you hurt your
body, your soul won't be hurt?
Are you choosing to inflict pain on yourself because
you can control what's happening to you?

Maybe it's none of those. I hear you. I get it. Let's try something. Imagine you're in a room and you're inviting that emotion in, whatever you are feeling in that moment. In doing so, you are welcoming that feeling instead of resisting, which brings compassion instead of judgement. The worst thing about a feeling is that you have to feel it in your body. That's it. No outside physical thing happens to you because you feel an emotion. It's the action that comes when you choose to act on that emotion. What if you just felt it in your body? Let's dig into that feeling.

Does it feel hot or cold?
Does it feel soft or hard?
Is it pointy or round?
Is it rough or smooth?
What color is it?
Where does it reside in your body?
Does it move or does it stay in one place? You can
breathe through that emotion, that feeling.
Do it with me right now.

Take a breath. In through the nose, out through the mouth. What's going on in your body right now? Asking that question brings so much awareness to your mind, like grounding techniques. Just notice and observe what's happening. No judgement, only curiosity. You can sit quietly in this moment and choose to take as much time as you need. I'll be here without judgement when you're ready to continue.

Once my friend so kindly told me, "You know Jen, I feel as though I can tell you anything and you won't judge," which I thought was such a wonderful compliment until she continued with, "Because you're always a hot mess."

At first, my instinct was to think "Wait a minute! I don't want to be a hot mess! I want to look like I am put together every minute of every day!"

Then I had a thought: I love that I am this way. This is perfect! Since one thing I always want to be is a safe space for women to share, I am 100% onboard the Hot Mess Express (maybe I need one of those mugs to fully cement this mantra) if it helps me create that space for other women. We all have our own versions of being a hot mess, it's just a matter of how well we are able to hide it. Me? Not good at all. Good ol' heart-on-the-sleeve kind of gal. I have accepted my fate.

So, go ahead take your time and remember, this "heart-on-the-sleeve, nonjudgmental" gal will be ready for you whenever you are.

Ok, ready to come back? Let's go.

How to take action and truly live

Even if you stop engaging in self-harm, you may still be preventing yourself from really living. You chose to live, but you aren't actually living. From experience, I know that sometimes feeling depression means you don't take action. If you are like me, you need a go-to list to get going. To see words in front of your eyeballs that give you an order of what to do right now when thinking seems challenging.

You can break it down even further if that helps. Instead of "take a shower," it could be "turn on water, take off clothes, step into shower." Whatever is needed for you to take that first step. Having things written down ahead of time before the depression episode starts is extremely helpful. It's having that preparation ready and waiting so you don't have to put more thought into what to do when your brain has shut down on a bad mental day. It takes the mental burden off of the decision of what to do next. Below, you'll see listed several things that might help when your brain decides to go all Looney Tunes. These things help me but, like I said before, they may not help you. However, maybe one or two will get the ol' wheels turning.

Tweak them, discard them, use them. You have the option to try whatever is helpful to shift the funk. If you have access to someone whom you trust, maybe share this list with them and see if they can encourage you to try some of these if you're not sure you can make yourself try them. This is what I call my "Depression Protocol." It's my go-to when things seem impossible and regular-life things seem unattainable. Since I usually struggle a lot more first thing in the morning, I am basing this list off of that. I have listed it below, but I have also included it in the back of the book for quick reference.

Depression Protocol

- Take care of the other creatures in my house
  - In my case, fill dog's food and water bowls, let her outside
- Drink coffee
  - Or tea or an adrenal cocktail (orange juice, coconut water or ¼ tsp. cream of tartar, ¼ tsp. sea salt) or something delicious that gets you out of bed

- Sit in shower
  - o Sometimes cold water helps jolt you awake and get the blood flowing, but hot water helps soothe for the most part. And I definitely take my homemade latte in the shower with me. I mean, people have shower beer, so why not shower lattes?? COFFEE DRINKERS UNITE.
- Brush your hair
  - o This goes along with the shower. One big thing about helping support ourselves through depression is taking care of our physical body when we don't want to do it. If you have dreadlocks, or some other hairstyle that isn't conducive to brushing, do one thing that cares for your hair.
- Put on CLEAN clothes
  - o I can't tell you how much of a difference this makes. Pick something you feel cute in.
- Fill up water bottle
  - o Hydration helps clear the mind; if it's filtered, that's even better!
- Fill essential-oil diffusers
  - o I used to light candles 24/7 and then did some research. For those who have hardcore depression, or even light-core depression, fake fragrances increase depression symptoms.
- Pick a hobby to focus on for 20 minutes
  - o If that's too many minutes, try 10, or even 5. Put on a timer. What makes you feel passionate on a good mental day? What makes you feel alive? If you don't know yet, that's okay. Take your time and explore the

next time you have a good mental day. Lots of experimenting.

- Sit in direct sunshine for 20 minutes
  - o Or get one of those light things from Amazon. I am fortunate enough to live in a place with direct sunlight on most days, so I get the benefit of free light!
- Sit in fresh air for 20 minutes
  - o It may be the dead of winter, but you always have the option to bundle yourself up and go outside for even a few minutes. The cold air might even help wake you up!
- Eat a breakfast that has protein, fat, and carbs
  - o I know you may not be hungry and food may look gross right now, but digesting food will help kick the bod into gear. If you are able to eat whole foods instead of processed, even better. This is part of nurturing your body, which, in turn, helps your mind. (think eggs, fruit, avocado, toast)
- Take pills
  - o Anxiety meds, depression meds, or supplements. Even if you feel like you don't deserve to feel better, or you don't think they are working, take them today anyway. The next good mental day you can always go to the doctor and see if there are better meds that can help you. Don't stop taking them on a bad day because you have a bad day.
- Put on happy music
  - o E.g., Mamma Mia or The Paper Kites. Music has such an impact on the brain without us consciously acknowledging that. What

makes you want to dance? What makes you want to sing along?

- Move the bod!
  - o What kind of movement do you like to do? Is it a walk outside in the fresh air? Is it some stretching or yoga/breathwork? Is it dancing around the house to that happy music? Pushups? Squats? You pick. What is the easiest movement you can do in this moment?
- Journal
  - o I hesitate to put this on the list since this is definitely a hit or miss. Sometimes, dumping out all of your feelings and thoughts about how you are feeling in that moment is therapeutic. Sometimes, all it does is get you more entrenched inside your head. I usually save this one for when I'm feeling a wee bit more loosey-goosey.
- Meditation
  - o Pick a depression-based meditation. Thanks to the internet, all you have to do is go to YouTube and presto! So many options from which to choose! Sit with your legs up against the wall with your back flat on the floor. This helps with blood flow and, bonus, you're still lying down! Hearing someone else's voice leading you through thoughts and focusing on your body enables release and forces focus on something else other than our depression.

Now, you might do all of these things (or your own personalized list) and it might not completely work. Totally fine. Maybe today is a day for lots of compassion and maybe you do need to just stare at something for a bit (but maybe exile the bedroom). One boundary that I put in place for myself is I don't eat/drink in bed anymore and, if I need to sit and stare at the wall, I am only allowed to do that outside my bedroom. It's helped dissipate the unintentional habit that was forming that every time I went into my bedroom, I wanted to lay on the bed and stare at the wall or sleep. I save my bedroom for sleeping at night.

You might have those days. Give yourself permission for the grace, for the compassion that you would show to someone else struggling with this. Remember, we don't punish ourselves anymore for having depression. We can choose that space and time to take a moment and be gentle with ourselves. As we make the transition from discussing depression to discussing PTSD, let's remember that these two are linked with a common need to build a relationship with ourselves and learning to trust what we need in that moment.

Chapter 7

THE UGLINESS OF SEXUAL ASSAULT

Note: Please know, while I will focus on reporting men for improper conduct, I fully recognize that women sometimes are sexually inappropriate as well. I do not have personal experience with women, only men; therefore, I will continue to refer to only men in these situations.

This is the subject I feel the most passionate about in my life. From being touched inappropriately as a child, to being sexually harassed in every job I've had since 15 years old, to being raped by men I thought were my friends, this is an important topic to me. I know my life is not an exception; these things are commonplace in this world, and it's not okay. The majority of men who have done these things to me call themselves Christians. Please know, these men do not represent Christ. That is not what Jesus teaches. And it is not okay how you were treated.

At times, I didn't realize how messed up some of those experiences were until the situation passed. And then my brain pops up with the realization I was sexually harassed, but our culture has become so hardened to this kind of behavior that it becomes acceptable; it's not acceptable. Maybe, as we move forward, the number of men who treat women with respect will increase. In the meantime, I can keep speaking up for myself and for those who are unable to speak for themselves. I didn't start until I came back from South Sudan—where I lived and worked for a year. It taught me that if I could handle all I experienced over there, then I can start reporting men who are dangerous.

As a side note, it's a tough line to walk, and so much responsibility to put on girls who have been taught to listen to, and respect, authority, and yet, women of all ages are also automatically expected to recognize and confront fully grown men who are perverts.

Reporting sexual assault

Reporting assault is a whole different kind of monster, and I fully recognize this isn't for everyone. Maybe this seems disjointed to be talking about reporting in a book about trauma, but it's about building that relationship with ourselves, learning to trust ourselves, and listen to ourselves again. Reporting someone who assaults you can be part of that process. When we take that step of writing down the statement of what someone has done to you and make it public, you are saying to yourself, and others, that you believe what happened to you is wrong. You are standing up for yourself and saying that something needs to be done, because actions have consequences. You are saying that whatever happened was not your fault. All of these things stem from trusting yourself. Sometimes, as with depression and a whole host of other mental diagnoses, we hand over our power of how we feel to others. Reporting can be one way to take that power back and claim it for ourselves. In doing that, we are retraining our brain to trust ourselves and, in doing so, we are able to make better decisions for ourselves in a difficult moment. But, before we move on, I want to hammer home that if you never report, it doesn't mean you don't believe the above sentences. Reporting is an option for you, not a requirement. If you choose never to report anything, that doesn't mean anything bad about you.

As I write this, there is still an assault I have not reported and I'm not sure if I ever will. If this section is triggering you, skip it and move to the next section. If you are fearful of reporting but still want to know more, keep reading.

Yes, sometimes, when you get the courage to report or confront someone regarding inappropriate sexual conduct or, heck, even something that makes you feel uncomfortable, the person responds with, "It's part of my culture/religion," or, "That's just my personality," or the person you're reporting to offers excuses for them. None of these excuses are valid. Absolutely none of them. I don't care if they proclaim, "I'm a hugger!" All that means is they aren't willing to listen to the other person, and they only care about their wants in that moment.

I experienced these comments when I confronted this kind of behavior. One of them was my Kenyan supervisor in South Sudan. He made several inappropriate comments and I had enough, so I reported him. I was told, "It's the African culture." Another man gave unsolicited shoulder massages, and another man screamed whenever things didn't go his way. I was told, "That's just his personality," and I "needed to deal with it." If you ever find yourself in a situation like this, I hope you see that you can always leave. I didn't feel like I had a choice in that moment because I didn't think I was right. I kept second guessing myself and telling myself I was being too this or too that. Those thoughts, dear reader, are a total lie. You don't have to put up with that. Is that hard? Absolutely.

Especially when your brain has been practicing the exact opposite for years and we have people outside ourselves also telling us we are being too sensitive. I get it; I've been told these lies since I was a kid. But we can do it. If I can start making little steps like this, you can too.

Now, did I automatically flip a switch and, presto, I immediately report when a man harasses me? Of course not. My brain was still getting used to the different script, a new train track of, *"Ok, now we don't tolerate harassment. Now, we report when we are harassed."* I was scared and maybe you are too. My first test came when I was volunteering as an EMT and an older, "respected" adult decided to touch me and say disgusting things to me. At first, I was scared of the consequences. His son was the one in charge; I knew this older man had gotten away with this behavior in the past. I knew I would be the one to be blamed, but then I found out he had done the same things to another underage girl I am close to. Then came the rage, which overshadowed the fear. And then I found out that he's been doing this for years. So, I spoke up. I wrote a very professional report and submitted it. Of course, women who have been assaulted or harassed are not allowed to be emotional about trauma or the courts will call us hysterical, but we also can't be too stoic or they will say we don't care. Gotta love that lose-lose situation. You need to be emotional to be believed, but you can't be too emotional. (Insert eye roll here.) At first, it was incredibly discouraging. He had "boundaries," such as he wasn't allowed in the building without an approved supervisor, but since I saw him in the building by himself, I knew they weren't enforced. I reported that too, but was ignored. But then, I heard that someone else came forward and since he had several written complaints submitted, he was FINALLY removed from his leadership position.

Another time, I wasn't going to report, but once I heard another girl was too scared to come forward, I did. Now, he was in the government, so he didn't have any consequences at all, just a transfer. But, still, he was out of direct leadership from us. Gosh, that's pretty sad, celebrating something like that. But little steps, right? To be honest, I'm still frustrated and tempted to feel helpless at times. After all, depression loves these types of situations, as it points out the things in our lives that seem hopeless and files that "evidence" away in our file cabinet of life isn't worth living. It can feel hopeless when it seems like nothing ever happens. It's like we need to have multiple complaints (aka establishing a pattern of behavior before anything at all even happens). But, if women started reporting it, then we would start establishing that pattern of behavior. And maybe, just maybe, we can start getting those men out of leadership and holding them accountable.

Learn to trust who is safe and who isn't

Please keep in mind that men, as a category, are not dangerous. Are certain men dangerous? Sure. In the same way, some women are dangerous, but not all women. The trixy part is differentiating the dangerous men from those who will not physically hurt me. (This is something through which I am still working.) Be observant when the alarm bells go off and see if there is actual danger. Focus on the man in front of you instead of keeping that individual in the overall "threatening" group. Is this man making you uncomfortable? You can believe that gut feeling, that vibe. Let's build that trust in ourselves; that we know exactly what we need in that moment. You can choose to get away in the moment and process later. Later, we can sit down and literally ask ourselves these questions like we are talking to a friend, "Hey, what's going on? What was going through my brain? Was it something he actually did or was it his cologne that reminded me of a previous assault?"

Once we build that trust in ourselves, it will become easier to differentiate between a real emergency and one that our brains only present as one. If that doesn't make sense right now, that's okay. It's all part of the process of us learning how to work with our PTSD and our depression and anxiety in order to have a better life than if we didn't struggle with these things. I'm still learning and am trekking right along with you on this journey, using each trigger to see how to improve my self-trust. All of the things in our lives cause us to work on our reactions to our struggles. Our trauma doesn't make us stronger, the reaction to our trauma does. We can seek to grow in how we respond and make our lives better than what we ever imagined. And, sometimes, even with us growing and changing and learning, we have those moments that make us feel like we are going back to square one where the triggers seem like they are increasing, or the suicidal thoughts come dashing in and have a party in our brain. I know these thoughts may seem scary, but we can learn to work with them and be okay with them coming into our brains.

Navigating life and intimacy after sexual assault

As I mentioned in the beginning of this book, I was assaulted twice in my 20s. What I didn't realize until I was diagnosed several years after the attacks was I had PTSD as a result. Because of the way my brain was rewired, I began making decisions that didn't make any sense to anyone but me. Sometimes those decisions hurt people in my life and, at other times, it hurt only myself. An example of the latter: I would go on dates with guys with whom I didn't want to spend time because I was terrified that if I said no, then I would be raped again. When it seemed obvious that the guy wanted sex (which was, let's be real, every time I went on a date), it was like my brain automatically played one sentence like a CD on repeat: Do whatever you want. Sometimes, my brain muttered this to myself and my body went limp and numb, just resigned to get it over with. Sometimes, it was fearful and anxious, like my body was saying I will do anything he wants, but just don't hurt me. Just don't kill me.

One time, I found out the guy I was making out with was into choking. When he started choking me, I was terrified at first, but then all I could think was, "I hope he kills me. Maybe this is the end." Imagine my disappointment when I woke up from blacking out and I was still alive. And yet, there was something in my brain, in my body that wanted me to live. Wanted me to survive.

You've survived whatever has been in your life previously. You're here. There must be a reason. It really is ironic that, even in those moments when you want to die, to have that pain and fear erased, something in your body resisted. Something inside you raised its head and insisted, "I DO want to live." Your body's survival instincts kicked in to help prevent additional tearing, pain, or death. It's crazy, and maybe a little interesting, to think about the body's mechanisms for protection. (I waver on this thought sometimes. Sometimes I am able to access the thought that it's interesting and, other times, not so much.) For example, your body releases fluid during a rape to help prevent as much pain as it can. Of course, then your brain tries to convince you since you weren't completely dry, you actually did like it and leave you to question if you were actually assaulted. There go the body's protective mechanisms turning your brain against you again. It's difficult sometimes to parse through what is real and what is a protective mechanism that your brain is convinced you need to survive.

This is part of what makes navigating life after assault so difficult. Then, if you add an intimate relationship to your life, you have to face even more difficulties. At the risk of boring you regarding my wonderful husband, I want to tell you more about him, but probably not for the reason you think. Sure, our marriage is intimate and has romance and lovey-doveyness, but to me it's first and foremost based on our friendship. And what is friendship based on? Trust. My husband has become one of my best friends and a safe space for me and alllll my human emotions. But, of course, having sex with one of your best friends adds a whole other level of complication and necessity to increase communication.

Intimacy is especially complicated when you have trauma/PTSD from past sexual assault inflicted by someone of the same gender you are attempting to have a good and healthy sex life with now. Even if the assault came from another gender, triggers do still happen and it's completely normal and expected.

Learning how to feel safe during sex after assault/trauma definitely requires processing. Something innocuous that seems like a "normal" part of sex to some can send my mind into a downward spiral, make my brain shut down, and cause everything inside me to curl into the figurative fetal position. Meanwhile, my brain sends what it thinks is a protective thought through my head. Maybe the sentence that continually runs through your head is different than mine or maybe it's similar to the one that I think when my brain shuts down: "Do whatever you want, just do whatever you want."

Unfortunately, your brain comes barreling in like a bull in a china shop with extremely unhelpful alerts when nothing is actually happening. (I.e., trying to have sex with your significant other where you are, in actuality, completely safe, but your brain is shouting at you the exact opposite.) Like alarm bells going off when, in fact, there is no emergency, leaving the logical side of the brain, the "higher brain," if you will, to determine fact from fiction. In that moment, when your brain thinks your survival is threatened, it goes into pure "fight-or-flight." That higher side of your brain is now nowhere to be found. All logic goes out the window. But that's the brain's job: keep us alive. As much as I get annoyed at my brain, and want to tell it to shut its pie hole when it's trying to convince me a nonexistent emergency is real, we don't need to be mad at our brain. Remember, our brains are silly pickles. When our brains are focused on making sure we survive, that alarm trigger gets a wee bit too sensitive. We always have the option to acknowledge our brains, thank them for looking out for us, and tell them we've got it from here. We have new tools that we can use. We have new knowledge that we can apply to the situation. We are not on that past train track anymore.

You have to find the tools and knowledge that work for you. For some, they can change their thoughts in the moment and think, "I am safe now." That doesn't work for me. I usually focus on what is actually happening, breaking everything into small, little facts, such as, *"I am standing," "The floor is concrete," "A man is standing in front of me,"* or, *"I am holding a cup."* If neither of these suggestions work for you, don't fret! That's the beautiful thing about us humans; we are all different and can come up with so many awesome ideas to help ourselves process in the moment! Try on other thoughts, or ideas of how to process what is happening, like a hat, and see how it lands in your brain. If this one doesn't work, try another. Sometimes it takes time and fourteen tries, and that's perfect because you've got time. All the time in the world. No rush. And the best part is, since we have an abundance of time, we have the time to practice how to respond in the moment when we are triggered. Ready to move forward? Let's move on to the next page and keep going.

Chapter 8

PTSD, Anxiety and Martial Arts

*A*nother unexpected consequence of living by myself in a pandemic was the collection of thoughts that rushed into my mind from memories of my time living and working for over a year in South Sudan. As I mentioned before, I didn't have my community yet in Arlington. So, day in and day out, as the only human in the house, I started having flashbacks to living in South Sudan behind barbed wire, in a place where I was not safe. A classic symptom of PTSD.

And the January 6th, 2021 incident, where a mob of people stormed the US Capitol, turned up that dial to an 11. Living in a war zone did some weird things to my mind, even though I was only in a war zone for little over a year. In my mind, since DC was only 15 minutes from my house, I was in danger (or so shouted my brain). It brought back to mind the time I was staying in Maban where there was a hostage situation a few minutes down the road at another compound. The fences at our compound were falling down and our guards were never allowed weapons. So, we were basically screwed if they decided to come our way. That feeling of "there's nothing I can do, I can't get out" is a terrible one. If you've felt that feeling before, then you too know how paralyzing it can be. It's a kind of fear that envelops and overwhelms, making your brain shut down and focus on just the very basic survival goals.

When you have PTSD or anxiety, you can get triggered by innocuous things, and you need a way to combat that.

Your brain and body's reaction

When you are triggered, even when you're technically safe, your body reacts and your fight-or-flight-or-freeze kicks in. It's lovely timing, but it makes sense. It's trying to save you. My choice reaction is freeze. My breathing becomes shallow and panicked, my body becomes heavy and unmoving and I. Just. Freeze.

Some of you may get this since this is your reaction, others have no clue what I am talking about, that's okay. You know exactly how your own body responds to triggers like these, even in controlled settings. What I'm getting at is these responses are all normal and they make so much sense, as frustrating as they may be. I certainly don't want to be freezing while I am going about normal life activities or breaking down into tears when my brain decides that fear will win instead of confidence. But, if your brain does this to you as well, our brains are convinced that this will help us survive. And, guess what, even though those responses are unwanted right now, they HAVE helped you survive because you are here reading this book right now. They worked and, because they worked, the brain filed that information away for future use. I know, I know, it may seem dumb. But, you are alive because of that reaction. Even though you may have been assaulted or beaten or impregnated, and have lasting consequences from that person's actions, YOU ARE ALIVE.

Can we take a moment and thank our body for keeping us alive up to this moment? If you're not able to do that, and need to be angry/upset for a while longer, that's okay. This is your life, and you get to decide how to process through the emotions you are feeling and the trauma that has happened to you.

If you're ready, thank your body right now for keeping you alive. To those who have rolled their eyes reading that, it absolutely may seem super ridiculous and all kinds of woo-woo, but it helps. It enables your brain to relax when you acknowledge what is going on in your body. Your brain is shouting at you for a reason; let's not punish it for doing its job. Let's continue to build that relationship between your body and brain and start working together instead of creating opposition.

Creating a powerful persona

While I focus on Jiu Jitsu and how to react in moments of panic while sparring with someone, you can also use these suggestions for those times in life when you are having a trigger. When you are triggered, slow your breathing, notice what's around you, and listen to yourself. Your brain isn't going to turn off unless you acknowledge the alarm first. Your brain is trying to get you to pay attention to it, and if you continue to push it down, it will be like a pushing a beach ball underwater. The pressure will continue to increase until it's too much and it pops above the water. Sometimes, your brain will calm down once you acknowledge the alarm and you'll be able to recover and continue on with whatever you are doing. But, sometimes it won't, especially if you are new to rewiring your neuropathways, and that's okay. Maybe that's a time you need to leave the situation and take some breaths or cry in your car or at home. It's still helping because you are acknowledging and building that trust relationship with your brain.

It's important you learn to feel safe, which means you are either no longer triggered, or you learn how to handle the trigger. I have always been a taller and bigger-boned person and, at 6-feet tall, you would think that I would feel safe on a day-to-day basis. That is a big HELL TO THE NAH. The height and weight of my physical body has not determined how safe I feel and I did not start feeling safe until this year. Jiu Jitsu helped me feel safe. It has been one crazy ride of an experience and a learning process. But, after wading through all the stuff that Jiu Jitsu throws at you, I am starting to feel safe when I am out by myself. I have had moments where a man is approaching me on the street and I start staring him down with the thought of, "Try it, let's go, moron." That thought had never occurred to me before this year. Of course, I am not saying everyone needs to sprint to their nearest dojo and sign up for a 10-year membership. But, something about knowing you could protect yourself the next time someone approaches you creates this atmosphere of confidence, as if you're encased in a bubble. If anyone broaches that bubble, you get to show them you're not someone to be messed with. You get to discover for yourself that you can diffuse a situation or escape or choke them out if need be. Or, heck, just break their arm. That might distract them for a bit.

Jiu Jitsu enables you to create a powerful persona that others recognize, especially predators because they are looking for an easy target. This doesn't just have to just apply to Jiu Jitsu either; I am specifically talking about Jiu Jitsu since I have personal experience. But, you can make this your own. What hobby would enable you to develop a persona of confidence and power?

When I asked my therapist why I was a continual target for people who have harassed/assaulted me, she explained that they knew I wouldn't put up a fight, that I would hand over the power to them. At first, I blamed myself (that seems to be the go-to for us depression types, right?), but there's nothing to blame myself for and that is NOT the point of this at all. The blame for things that happened to me (and you) belongs firmly with the perpetrator. And now, armed with this information, I can change my persona and create the feeling of safety and confidence to deter future attacks. If that doesn't work, and future attacks occur, I have those tools to protect myself and get out of the situation without repeating the cycle from the last one.

With whichever method you use to help change your persona and create confidence, you want to practice it in a safe environment because your brain will still react, and you will need to retrain it.

Retraining your brain

Practicing in a safe environment won't prevent you from being triggered, but it gives you a safe place to practice dealing with your PTSD triggers. For example, in sparring with white belt (beginner) males, who tend to use brute force and "smashing" instead of controlled pressure and technique, I was triggered. My body doesn't recognize, or care, that I was in a safe and "controlled" environment.

Remember, our body, like our brain, is all about our survival. It doesn't know that we are in a class where we are choosing to get ourselves smashed by someone who weighs over 50 pounds more than us. It doesn't know that we are actively trying to teach ourselves how to respond in stressful situations. All it knows is there is a huge man lying on top of us and a light bulb (or, more accurately, a huge freaking alarm bell) clicks on and the brain starts screaming, "Hey wait, we know this! We've been in this place before, we don't want to be in this place again! Look what happened last time, what are you doing, we don't want to be here!" I probably should have put that in all caps because that voice truly is screaming at us to DO SOMETHING. ANYTHING. And this doesn't just apply to Jiu Jitsu; it could be any situation that reminds us of previous trauma. Sometimes, it's as simple as making eye contact with someone that reminds us of our attacker and then here comes a freight train of a reaction.

Once you acknowledge the warning signs, you can gently tell your brain that you've got this. For example, you're rolling with a huge, male white belt, and he is smashing the ever-living daylights out of you. Everything starts getting smaller, your breathing is becoming more rapid, and your brain starts shouting at you to GET OUT. What now?

In the Jiu Jitsu world, it would go something like this: slow your breathing, get your elbow-knee connection to make space, push up your frames to make space, and continue to slow your breathing. Next, plan your sweep or escape or whatever you can do to switch positions and follow through.

Let's broaden that view to those who never want to step foot in a dojo: slow your breathing, take notice of your surroundings, practice some grounding techniques: what are five things you can see, four things you can touch, three things you can hear, and two things you can smell. And the cherry on top: another way to calm your brain is to pretend you just licked a lemon. Try it. If you have typical taste buds, and have tasted a lemon before, your mouth will automatically create saliva since it is a sour fruit, which in turn tells your body it's safe since a release of saliva lets your body know it's time to eat.

If it isn't available to you in that moment, you can "tap" (when you tap your opponent's body to let them know you concede, and you start over in the original sparring position). What does "tapping" look like in real life? There are a few options to reset your brain. Maybe put your back against a wall and take a moment. Maybe you can get to your car and release your emotions with tears. Maybe you can put on a song that is the opposite of what you are feeling in this moment. Ask yourself what resets your brain. This is where more experimenting comes in, and really getting to know yourself is key. All of this takes time and practice. Practice seems too light of a word. Since you are literally rewiring your neuropathways, it's going to take a bit. In the meantime, if you feel yourself going into survival mode, tap. There's no shame in tapping in sparring or in real-life situations. And, tapping quickly each time will help your brain start to know that you can get out of this situation whenever you choose. You are not trapped, like your brain is thinking you are. You can decide when you want out, when you want to stop. That's a choice that we didn't have during the traumatic experience, but we have that choice now.

Let's choose to practice that often. It's one of the first steps we can take to start building that relationship of trust between our brain and body, to take back the power over our decisions that we have given to others. We do have the option to practice choosing for ourselves. We don't have to allow others to keep that power for themselves. Let's take that back. They're not allowed to have that anymore.

Chapter 9

INTERVIEW WITH MY LOVER
IN THE NIGHTTIME

*A*s the final chapter, I wanted to address those who are reading this book because they have a loved one who has depression or PTSD, or maybe even anxiety. I hope this book has given you a bit of understanding or some ideas of encouraging things to say or do when your loved one is in the middle of an episode. Here is an interview I did with my husband, providing his point of view of living with a mentally ill person, yours truly!

There are also some bits of information for us mentally-ill type of peeps reading this book as it's good to hear from a perspective looking in at our diagnosis from the outside. Many times, as you know, the depression gets heavy enough to convince us that our significant other or our friends are tired of our depression or that we stress them out, annoy them, or any other thing that our brain throws at us to keep us entrenched in our depression. This was helpful to me (and hopefully for you) to hear, a lot of the time, that is not what they are thinking. They just aren't sure what to do when someone they love is struggling hard-core. Hopefully, this can dispel some of the lies that our not so helpful pickle of a brain tells us.

> **Note:** The entire time we were talking, dogs were being walked past our front window and I was hard-pressed to ignore them (and not point them out to my husband) as not to disrupt my husband's train of thought. I succeeded, but just barely.

--------- **Interview** ---------

Okay, in your experience, what is it like living with someone who has been diagnosed with depression and PTSD?

That's a very broad question.

I figured I'd start easy.

I'd say some days are easier than others. I think the easy days are just normal days. We both do our thing and the days are great. I think the tough days are when you have a depressive episode. Those days are tough because I bounce between feeling anxious and feeling useless. I don't feel like I can say the right things or do the right things. It's not like I can bring you a bowl of soup and a blanket and make everything better. I don't know if there's anything I can do on those days. The challenge is finding the small things I can do to support you when you're going through that, whether it's making you eat when you haven't eaten all day or if it's just being there and hanging out in the same room to be a presence while you're working through the mental aspects of it. I think it's been small incremental changes of how can I support you and honor you while, at the same time, honestly, supporting and caring for myself. Because, at the end of the day, if I come home and I am stressed out of my mind and completely empty and I need all these things and you're having a really bad depression day, I can't help you. I need to take care of me first to be able to take care of you as well. It's finding that balance between being a supportive and caring partner and finding ways to make sure I am good as well. I have to understand that I can't magically fix things and there's not a magic word I can say, or just hand you a bowl of ice cream and it's suddenly sunshine and rainbows. I've seen the improvements you've made for yourself and to me that's encouraging because you are working to take care of your mental health. So, if you're putting in the work to be a better you, I want to put in the work to be a better me, and a better partner.

What would you say to those that feel like a burden to their significant others and think that if they weren't around, their SO's life would be so much better?

I would say a couple things. The first is that you don't always see the impact you make in their lives, but I can guarantee that it's there. We do a tremendously horrible job at showing someone how much value their life has for us sometimes. Often, your life is like the warmth of the sun. We enjoy it, we feel it around us, but we don't always actively notice it. When it's gone though, the world feels cold and harsh. So, I can promise that however much of a burden you may feel sometimes, you would be missed dearly. The second thing is that we so often focus on the things we don't like about ourselves, whereas our significant others see the things they love about us. So, you may feel like a burden, and you may feel like you don't matter, that you're too this or that but, I can guarantee that your SO sees you in a wonderful light. Something that has helped me when I struggle with my sense of self-worth is putting myself in the shoes of my wife and trying to see myself how she sees me. It doesn't always immediately fix everything but it often gives me enough strength to press forward until I can see myself that way. I would encourage anyone struggling with depression to do the same. There is someone (probably many someones) out there who care deeply about you, and they certainly don't view you as a burden.

What's the worst thing about being with someone with depression and PTSD?

I think it's feeling helpless. It's feeling like there isn't something I can do to fix it and feeling guilty because I wish I could just do something to make it go away. And then I feel guilty because I'm trying to fix you instead of loving you like I should and it almost feels like I'm trying to change this part of you, even though I imagine you don't want to live a life with depression. Even just thinking "I wish she didn't have to deal with that." It's easy to go from that to feeling like I'm trying to change this part of you. I fell in love with someone with depression. Part of me feels like, if I try too hard to change certain aspects of your life, even if they're something like depression, I would lose that person I fell in love with. I want to find a balance between encouraging you and giving you the space you need. But, all that stuff is easier to deal with. It's the feelings of guilt that come from knowing it's a long-term struggle and won't get better overnight, and that sounds like a lot of work, but then realizing you've been dealing with it for a long time now, and how exhausted you must be. But, I know we are working toward making each day a little bit better. I know what works for me and for my anxiety. It's easier for me to accept that not all days for me are going to be good, but it's much more difficult to watch someone I love go through that kind of pain and mental exhaustion. It just sucks.

Do you ever get tired of dealing with me and my mental illness?

I wouldn't say get tired of dealing with it. I knew what I was agreeing to when I married you, and we've been together long enough that I had a pretty good idea of what the mental illness looked like. If I ever end up starting to venture into that thought of not wanting to deal with it, I kind of just remind myself you're the one actually battling it and you're the one it affects the most. My responsibility is to be supportive and be your partner. So, yeah, it's challenging, and some days are difficult, but I wouldn't say I get "tired" because, at the end of the day, my main focus is to be there and support you, mental illness or not. Being that support system for you is worth it; it's work and it's worth it. It's what it means to be in a relationship. And, I realize that I have my own stuff that you help me work through so, if I were to say, "This is too much to handle, too much to deal with," that's unfair because I have my own mess *that I'm working through. It's a commitment to continue to support each other through our messes.*

What would you say to people that have decided to read this book to get some understanding into someone's mind that has depression or PTSD?

I would say a couple things. The first thing is you won't have all the answers and you don't need to have them. You don't need to try to fix the person. Your job is to be supportive and be understanding. And, know that you probably won't be able to fully understand it. It's the idea of sympathy vs. empathy. You can sympathize with someone because you know what it's like to struggle with things, but you won't be able to empathize because you've never dealt with chronic depression. Mental illnesses are especially tricky because, unless you've dealt with it, you don't have the capacity to know what it's like, and that's okay. You don't need to know to support them. You can put yourself in their shoes as much as you're able but, at the end of the day, your job is to support them. The second thing I would say is: the best thing you can do is to just sit with somebody and just be there. It's not about saying the right things or doing the right things. Sometimes it's just being with somebody so that they know they're not alone.

I guess we kind of already talked about advice, but what is the number one piece of advice you would give to someone?

I think over the last few questions we kind of talked about it, but the biggest thing, especially when it comes to relationships, is it's really easy to take things personally. So, I would say try to not take things personally. Everyone has their own struggles, and mental illness can be particularly challenging. I relate a lot of this back to my struggle with anxiety. Sometimes, when I'm somewhere like a mall, I have episodes where I can't breathe and I freak out because

I'm surrounded by so many people and I feel trapped. I turn into a very different person. I get really short with people and I try to get away from the situation, and that has nothing to do with the people around me, other than that's just how I'm processing at the moment. When it comes to relationships, it's really hard because it feels like there's a wall in front of you and all you can see is a wall and you're just trying to get over it. Sometimes, that means you act in a way you don't want to act, and that's nothing against your significant other, you are just trying your best to navigate that situation. And going along with not taking things personally, taking your pride out of the equation. It's easy to get in your head and think, "If they just did this, then it would fix everything. If I was them, I would do this." Recognize that you are not that person and you are not dealing their burden and, even if you have dealt with depression, you are still a different person. Everyone deals with things differently. Things that help and work for you won't necessarily help or work for them. So, building your relationship with them on that foundation of "I want what's best for you" outside of what I think or feel is the right decision. That will lead to a place of being able to sympathize better and understand what they are going through by taking yourself out of the equation and looking at things more objectively.

Did anything change for you when you moved in with me? We had dated for a year and a half before you moved in; did anything change?

Yes, I think mostly in how we deal with things together. When we were dating, if you had a day where things were particularly bad, you could just say, "Hey, I'm having a really rough time, I need some space," and I wouldn't come over. So, living together is very different in that regard. I'm all up in your space. And then there is that helplessness piece, right? When you're having a bad day, I'm trying to figure out if you need space, but then there's a part of me that feels like I should be doing more. I didn't really have that when we were dating because you would say, "I need space," and I was like,

"Okay, cool, I'll talk to you tomorrow." But now, living together, it's that constant feeling of needing to do more. That's the biggest change that pops out, just being in close proximity all the time. It's not that I was sweeping it under the rug, but it's very different mentally. When you hear about it, you think, "That sucks and I'm sorry," but, when you actually see it, and you live around it every day, it's different. I want to do all the things to help you feel better.

Any final comments, questions, concerns, suggestions, recommendations, declarations, exclamations?

There's still a lot we don't understand about mental illness and there are still a lot of stigmas, so there are going to be a lot of people in this life who have their opinions of what you should do, how to live your life, and what help they should get and all these sorts of things. There will be days where this will feel overwhelming for them (those who struggle) and, by extension, feels overwhelming for you because everyone has their opinion of what this means and how to fix it. It's easy to overlook a lot of mental issues because we don't understand them. When someone is in "invisible" pain, it's a lot harder to see than if someone stubs their toe, for example. So, know that the stigma surrounding mental illness will likely always be there because people are genuinely incapable of understanding unless they have gone through it themselves. It's important to approach the subject with extra compassion and support, not make assumptions, and to try our best to understand what that person is going through and to support them going through that.

Well, thank you again for your time and answers and thanks for processing with me and loving me in this way.

He mouths "I love you" and makes a heart with his hands

Yes, we love to corn it up. It's one of the best parts of our marriage, all the corniness that ensues.

Conclusion

WHAT NEXT?

Okay, so you've made it to the end of the book, congratulations! I hope at least one sentence in this book was helpful to you. Writing this made me discover how far I have actually come. When you live with yourself day to day, sometimes it's easy to not notice everything that you have started doing for yourself, the ways you have improved, or decisions you've made today that you would not have dreamed of making several years ago. Or, maybe you feel like you've gotten worse over the past few years; that's okay.

Everyone starts somewhere. Maybe today can be your day to start the process of healing and coming back to who you are at your very core. I don't know what that looks like for you, but you do. If you read that sentence and thought you really don't know, I get that. I've been there, and I know it's challenging. But, once you start building that trust with yourself, things will start to appear that you never noticed before. Wherever you are in your journey right now, that is exactly where you are supposed to be in this moment. Welcome that thought with compassion and grace for yourself.

And now ask:

- Where do you want to go?
- Who do you want to be?
- What is the very next step you can make to start the journey towards the person you want to become?
- Does that mean therapy, getting outside and walking for a few minutes, getting off the couch and taking a shower, putting on clean clothes, or drinking a big glass of water?

You know you best. Maybe you aren't sure right now and that's ok. Keep going, keep thinking. If you give your brain a problem to solve, it will start working to answer it, even if you aren't aware of it at first. Let's take this one day at a time; and, when that seems too hard, take it one hour at a time. Once that hour is complete, only focus on the next hour. You've totally got this. We all do. I welcome you with all your humanness, emotions, and stuff. Nothing is wrong with you; we can make it. We will make it.

Appendix A

DEPRESSION PROTOCOL

- Take care of the other creatures in my house
    - In my case, fill dog's food and water bowls, let her outside
- Drink coffee
    - Or tea or an adrenal cocktail (orange juice, coconut water or ¼ tsp. cream of tartar, ¼ tsp. sea salt) or something delicious that gets you out of bed
- Sit in shower
    - Sometimes cold water helps jolt you awake and get the blood flowing, but hot water helps soothe for the most part. And I definitely take my homemade latte in the shower with me. I mean, people have shower beer, so why not shower lattes?? COFFEE DRINKERS UNITE.
- Brush your hair
    - This goes along with the shower. One big thing about helping support ourselves through depression is taking care of our physical body when we don't want to do

it. If you have dreadlocks, or some other hairstyle that isn't conducive to brushing, do one thing that cares for your hair.

- Put on CLEAN clothes
  - I can't tell you how much of a difference this makes. Pick something you feel cute in.
- Fill up water bottle
  - Hydration helps clear the mind; if it's filtered, that's even better!
- Fill essential-oil diffusers
  - I used to light candles 24/7 and then did some research. For those who have hardcore depression, or even light-core depression, fake fragrances increase depression symptoms.
- Pick a hobby to focus on for 20 minutes
  - If that's too many minutes, try 10, or even 5. Put on a timer. What makes you feel passionate on a good mental day? What makes you feel alive? If you don't know yet, that's okay. Take your time and explore the next time you have a good mental day. Lots of experimenting.
- Sit in direct sunshine for 20 minutes
  - Or get one of those light things from Amazon. I am fortunate enough to live in a place with direct sunlight on most days, so I get the benefit of free light!
- Sit in fresh air for 20 minutes
  - It may be the dead of winter, but you always have the option to bundle yourself up and go outside for even a few minutes. The cold air might even help wake you up!

- Eat a breakfast that has protein, fat, and carbs
  - I know you may not be hungry and food may look gross right now, but digesting food will help kick the bod into gear. If you are able to eat whole foods instead of processed, even better. This is part of nurturing your body, which, in turn, helps your mind. (think eggs, fruit, avocado, toast)
- Take pills
  - Anxiety meds, depression meds, or supplements. Even if you feel like you don't deserve to feel better, or you don't think they are working, take them today anyway. The next good mental day you can always go to the doctor and see if there are better meds that can help you. Don't stop taking them on a bad day because you have a bad day.
- Put on happy music
  - E.g., Mamma Mia or The Paper Kites. Music has such an impact on the brain without us consciously acknowledging that. What makes you want to dance? What makes you want to sing along?
- Move the bod!
  - What kind of movement do you like to do? Is it a walk outside in the fresh air? Is it some stretching or yoga/breathwork? Is it dancing around the house to that happy music? Pushups? Squats? You pick. What is the easiest movement you can do in this moment?
- Journal

- o I hesitate to put this on the list since this is definitely a hit or miss. Sometimes, dumping out all of your feelings and thoughts about how you are feeling in that moment is therapeutic. Sometimes, all it does is get you more entrenched inside your head. I usually save this one for when I'm feeling a wee bit more loosey-goosey.
- Meditation
  - o Pick a depression-based meditation. Thanks to the internet, all you have to do is go to YouTube and presto! So many options from which to choose! Sit with your legs up against the wall with your back flat on the floor. This helps with blood flow and, bonus, you're still lying down! Hearing someone else's voice leading you through thoughts and focusing on your body enables release and forces focus on something else other than our depression.

ACKNOWLEDGEMENTS

want to thank my husband for all of his encouragement and compassion and honesty. He has been my safe space since we began a relationship and has been one of my biggest cheerleaders.

To Adrienne and Anne for being my earliest readers of the rough draft for this book and encouraging me to pursue publishing. You both are always in my corner, no matter what, and I love you both so much!

To my Jiu Jitsu gals, who push me to be better and also are able to laugh while we are trying to choke each other out or break each other's arms, thank you for being you. For your encouragement and care and acceptance. Best sparring partners a gal could ask for.

And, I want to thank all of you for being here and for pushing through, for doing the "normal life" things that seem so difficult, but you still get up and keep going. I'd love for you to acknowledge that and celebrate yourself for how much strength that takes for you to keep going.

ABOUT THE AUTHOR

J en Perry is a kooky American who grew up in the redneck boonies of Southern Maryland. As a result of childhood trauma, she's had depression from a young age and added on suicidal thoughts, PTSD, and panic attacks to the mix over the years. Thanks to EMDR, hard work, and pomegranates, healing has taken place and she is well on her way to becoming a compassion expert. She recognized the need to create a safe space for those around her and wanted to put her own spin on the subject of mental health by writing about her own experience, injecting some humor to provide some levity in an otherwise dark subject. She loves fresh air, the smell of pine, and any activity that gets her outdoors with her husband, James, and her pit bull, Skye. And, of course, living a life that still has laughter and compassion and fun; embracing her depression instead of trying to run from or ignore it.

If this is a book that was helpful to you, this could also be helpful to someone you know. Maybe this would make a great birthday gift or a just a "I love you" gift for friends or family. Copies are available via print or eBook.

URGENT PLEA!

Thank You for Reading My Book!
I really appreciate all of your feedback and
I love hearing what you have to say.

I need your input to make the next version of this
book and my future books better. I want to be
able to reach as many people as possible with this
message and you can help that happen!

Please take two minutes now to leave a helpful review on
Amazon letting me know what you thought of the book

Thanks so much!

Jen